Sewing Log Book

AF366241

INFORMATION

NAME

ADDRESS

E-MAIL ADDRESS

WEBSITE

PHONE   **FAX**

EMERGENCY CONTACT PERSON

PHONE   **FAX**

Sewing Log Book

DETAILS

PROJECT ....

CREATED FOR ....

DATE STARTED .... DATE COMPLETED ....

ITEM .... QTY ....

PRICE .... DEPOSIT PAID .... BALANCE PAID ....

PATTERN USED ....

SUPPLIES NEEDED ....

SKETCH / PHOTO

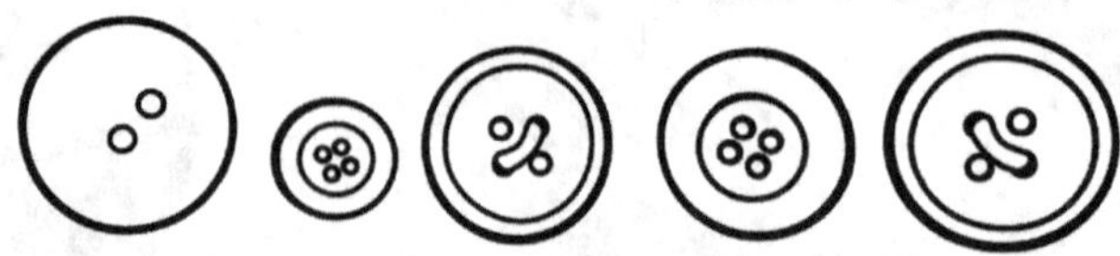

NOTES

....
....
....
....
....
....
....
....

Sewing Log Book

DETAILS

PROJECT ....

CREATED FOR ....

DATE STARTED .... DATE COMPLETED ....

ITEM .... QTY ....

PRICE .... DEPOSIT PAID .... BALANCE PAID ....

PATTERN USED ....

SUPPLIES NEEDED ....

SKETCH / PHOTO

NOTES

....
....
....
....
....
....
....
....

Sewing Log Book

DETAILS

PROJECT ....

CREATED FOR ....

DATE STARTED .... **DATE COMPLETED** ....

ITEM .... **QTY** ....

PRICE .... **DEPOSIT PAID** .... **BALANCE PAID** ....

PATTERN USED ....

SUPPLIES NEEDED ....

SKETCH / PHOTO

NOTES

....
....
....
....
....
....
....

Sewing Log Book

DETAILS

PROJECT ....

CREATED FOR ....

DATE STARTED .... DATE COMPLETED ....

ITEM .... QTY ....

PRICE .... DEPOSIT PAID .... BALANCE PAID ....

PATTERN USED ....

SUPPLIES NEEDED ....

SKETCH / PHOTO

NOTES

....
....
....
....
....
....
....

Sewing Log Book

PROJECT ....

CREATED FOR ....

DATE STARTED .... DATE COMPLETED ....

ITEM .... QTY ....

PRICE .... DEPOSIT PAID .... BALANCE PAID ....

PATTERN USED ....

SUPPLIES NEEDED ....

SKETCH / PHOTO

NOTES

....
....
....
....
....
....
....
....

Sewing Log Book

DETAILS

PROJECT ....

CREATED FOR ....

DATE STARTED .... **DATE COMPLETED** ....

ITEM .... **QTY** ....

PRICE .... **DEPOSIT PAID** .... **BALANCE PAID** ....

PATTERN USED ....

SUPPLIES NEEDED ....

SKETCH / PHOTO

NOTES

....
....
....
....
....
....
....
....

Sewing Log Book

DETAILS

PROJECT ....

CREATED FOR ....

DATE STARTED .... DATE COMPLETED ....

ITEM .... QTY ....

PRICE .... DEPOSIT PAID .... BALANCE PAID ....

PATTERN USED ....

SUPPLIES NEEDED ....

SKETCH / PHOTO

NOTES

....
....
....
....
....
....
....
....

Sewing Log Book

DETAILS

PROJECT ....

CREATED FOR ....

DATE STARTED .... DATE COMPLETED ....

ITEM .... QTY ....

PRICE .... DEPOSIT PAID .... BALANCE PAID ....

PATTERN USED ....

SUPPLIES NEEDED ....

SKETCH / PHOTO

NOTES

....
....
....
....
....
....
....

Sewing Log Book

DETAILS

PROJECT ....

CREATED FOR ....

DATE STARTED .... DATE COMPLETED ....

ITEM .... QTY ....

PRICE .... DEPOSIT PAID .... BALANCE PAID ....

PATTERN USED ....

SUPPLIES NEEDED ....

SKETCH / PHOTO

NOTES

....

....

....

....

....

....

....

Sewing Log Book

PROJECT ....

CREATED FOR ....

DATE STARTED .... DATE COMPLETED ....

ITEM .... QTY ....

PRICE .... DEPOSIT PAID .... BALANCE PAID ....

PATTERN USED ....

SUPPLIES NEEDED ....

....
....
....
....
....
....
....
....

Sewing Log Book

DETAILS

PROJECT ....

CREATED FOR ....

DATE STARTED .... DATE COMPLETED ....

ITEM .... QTY ....

PRICE .... DEPOSIT PAID .... BALANCE PAID ....

PATTERN USED ....

SUPPLIES NEEDED ....

SKETCH / PHOTO

NOTES

....
....
....
....
....
....
....
....

Sewing Log Book

DETAILS

PROJECT ....

CREATED FOR ....

DATE STARTED .... **DATE COMPLETED** ....

ITEM .... **QTY** ....

PRICE .... **DEPOSIT PAID** .... **BALANCE PAID** ....

PATTERN USED ....

SUPPLIES NEEDED ....

SKETCH / PHOTO

NOTES

....

....

....

....

....

....

....

Sewing Log Book

PROJECT ....

CREATED FOR ....

DATE STARTED .... DATE COMPLETED ....

ITEM .... QTY ....

PRICE .... DEPOSIT PAID .... BALANCE PAID ....

PATTERN USED ....

SUPPLIES NEEDED ....

....
....
....
....
....
....
....

Sewing Log Book

DETAILS

PROJECT ....

CREATED FOR ....

DATE STARTED .... **DATE COMPLETED** ....

ITEM .... **QTY** ....

PRICE .... **DEPOSIT PAID** .... **BALANCE PAID** ....

PATTERN USED ....

SUPPLIES NEEDED ....

SKETCH / PHOTO

NOTES

....
....
....
....
....
....
....

Sewing Log Book

PROJECT ....

CREATED FOR ....

DATE STARTED .... DATE COMPLETED ....

ITEM .... QTY ....

PRICE .... DEPOSIT PAID .... BALANCE PAID ....

PATTERN USED ....

SUPPLIES NEEDED ....

SKETCH / PHOTO

NOTES

....
....
....
....
....
....
....
....

Sewing Log Book

DETAILS

PROJECT ....

CREATED FOR ....

DATE STARTED .... **DATE COMPLETED** ....

ITEM .... **QTY** ....

PRICE .... **DEPOSIT PAID** .... **BALANCE PAID** ....

PATTERN USED ....

SUPPLIES NEEDED ....

SKETCH / PHOTO

NOTES

....
....
....
....
....
....
....

Sewing Log Book

DETAILS

PROJECT ....

CREATED FOR ....

DATE STARTED .... DATE COMPLETED ....

ITEM .... QTY ....

PRICE .... DEPOSIT PAID .... BALANCE PAID ....

PATTERN USED ....

SUPPLIES NEEDED ....

SKETCH / PHOTO

NOTES

....
....
....
....
....
....
....
....

Sewing Log Book

DETAILS

PROJECT ....

CREATED FOR ....

DATE STARTED .... DATE COMPLETED ....

ITEM .... QTY ....

PRICE .... DEPOSIT PAID .... BALANCE PAID ....

PATTERN USED ....

SUPPLIES NEEDED ....

SKETCH / PHOTO

NOTES

....
....
....
....
....
....
....

Sewing Log Book

PROJECT ....

CREATED FOR ....

DATE STARTED .... DATE COMPLETED ....

ITEM .... QTY ....

PRICE .... DEPOSIT PAID .... BALANCE PAID ....

PATTERN USED ....

SUPPLIES NEEDED ....

....
....
....
....
....
....
....

Sewing Log Book

DETAILS

PROJECT ....

CREATED FOR ....

DATE STARTED .... **DATE COMPLETED** ....

ITEM .... **QTY** ....

PRICE .... **DEPOSIT PAID** .... **BALANCE PAID** ....

PATTERN USED ....

SUPPLIES NEEDED ....

SKETCH / PHOTO

NOTES

....
....
....
....
....
....
....

Sewing Log Book

DETAILS

PROJECT ....

CREATED FOR ....

DATE STARTED .... DATE COMPLETED ....

ITEM .... QTY ....

PRICE .... DEPOSIT PAID .... BALANCE PAID ....

PATTERN USED ....

SUPPLIES NEEDED ....

SKETCH / PHOTO

NOTES

....
....
....
....
....
....
....

Sewing Log Book

PROJECT ....

CREATED FOR ....

DATE STARTED .... **DATE COMPLETED** ....

ITEM .... **QTY** ....

PRICE .... **DEPOSIT PAID** .... **BALANCE PAID** ....

PATTERN USED ....

SUPPLIES NEEDED ....

....
....
....
....
....
....
....

Sewing Log Book

DETAILS

PROJECT ....

CREATED FOR ....

DATE STARTED .... DATE COMPLETED ....

ITEM .... QTY ....

PRICE .... DEPOSIT PAID .... BALANCE PAID ....

PATTERN USED ....

SUPPLIES NEEDED ....

SKETCH / PHOTO

NOTES

....
....
....
....
....
....
....

Sewing Log Book

DETAILS

PROJECT ....

CREATED FOR ....

DATE STARTED .... DATE COMPLETED ....

ITEM .... QTY ....

PRICE .... DEPOSIT PAID .... BALANCE PAID ....

PATTERN USED ....

SUPPLIES NEEDED ....

SKETCH / PHOTO

NOTES

....
....
....
....
....
....
....

Sewing Log Book

DETAILS

PROJECT ....

CREATED FOR ....

DATE STARTED .... DATE COMPLETED ....

ITEM .... QTY ....

PRICE .... DEPOSIT PAID .... BALANCE PAID ....

PATTERN USED ....

SUPPLIES NEEDED ....

SKETCH / PHOTO

NOTES

....
....
....
....
....
....
....

Sewing Log Book

DETAILS

PROJECT ....

CREATED FOR ....

DATE STARTED .... DATE COMPLETED ....

ITEM .... QTY ....

PRICE .... DEPOSIT PAID .... BALANCE PAID ....

PATTERN USED ....

SUPPLIES NEEDED ....

SKETCH / PHOTO

NOTES

....
....
....
....
....
....
....

Sewing Log Book

PROJECT ....

CREATED FOR ....

DATE STARTED .... DATE COMPLETED ....

ITEM .... QTY ....

PRICE .... DEPOSIT PAID .... BALANCE PAID ....

PATTERN USED ....

SUPPLIES NEEDED ....

Sewing Log Book

DETAILS

PROJECT ....

CREATED FOR ....

DATE STARTED .... DATE COMPLETED ....

ITEM .... QTY ....

PRICE .... DEPOSIT PAID .... BALANCE PAID ....

PATTERN USED ....

SUPPLIES NEEDED ....

SKETCH / PHOTO

NOTES

....
....
....
....
....
....
....
....

Sewing Log Book

DETAILS

PROJECT ....

CREATED FOR ....

DATE STARTED .... DATE COMPLETED ....

ITEM .... QTY ....

PRICE .... DEPOSIT PAID .... BALANCE PAID ....

PATTERN USED ....

SUPPLIES NEEDED ....

SKETCH / PHOTO

NOTES

....
....
....
....
....
....
....

Sewing Log Book

DETAILS

PROJECT ....

CREATED FOR ....

DATE STARTED .... **DATE COMPLETED** ....

ITEM .... **QTY** ....

PRICE .... **DEPOSIT PAID** .... **BALANCE PAID** ....

PATTERN USED ....

SUPPLIES NEEDED ....

SKETCH / PHOTO

NOTES

....
....
....
....
....
....

Sewing Log Book

PROJECT ....

CREATED FOR ....

DATE STARTED .... **DATE COMPLETED** ....

ITEM .... **QTY** ....

PRICE .... **DEPOSIT PAID** .... **BALANCE PAID** ....

PATTERN USED ....

SUPPLIES NEEDED ....

....
....
....
....
....
....
....

Sewing Log Book

DETAILS

PROJECT ……………………………………………………………

CREATED FOR ……………………………………………………

DATE STARTED ………………………… DATE COMPLETED ……………………

ITEM ……………………………………… QTY ……………………

PRICE ………………… DEPOSIT PAID ……………… BALANCE PAID ……………

PATTERN USED ……………………………………………………

SUPPLIES NEEDED ………………………………………………

SKETCH / PHOTO

NOTES

……………………………………………………………………………
……………………………………………………………………………
……………………………………………………………………………
……………………………………………………………………………
……………………………………………………………………………
……………………………………………………………………………
……………………………………………………………………………

Sewing Log Book

PROJECT ....

CREATED FOR ....

DATE STARTED .... DATE COMPLETED ....

ITEM .... QTY ....

PRICE .... DEPOSIT PAID .... BALANCE PAID ....

PATTERN USED ....

SUPPLIES NEEDED ....

....
....
....
....
....
....
....

Sewing Log Book

DETAILS

PROJECT ....

CREATED FOR ....

DATE STARTED .... **DATE COMPLETED** ....

ITEM .... **QTY** ....

PRICE .... **DEPOSIT PAID** .... **BALANCE PAID** ....

PATTERN USED ....

SUPPLIES NEEDED ....

SKETCH / PHOTO

NOTES

....
....
....
....
....
....
....
....

Sewing Log Book

DETAILS

PROJECT ....

CREATED FOR ....

DATE STARTED .... DATE COMPLETED ....

ITEM .... QTY ....

PRICE .... DEPOSIT PAID .... BALANCE PAID ....

PATTERN USED ....

SUPPLIES NEEDED ....

SKETCH / PHOTO

NOTES

....
....
....
....
....
....
....

Sewing Log Book

DETAILS

PROJECT ....

CREATED FOR ....

DATE STARTED .... DATE COMPLETED ....

ITEM .... QTY ....

PRICE .... DEPOSIT PAID .... BALANCE PAID ....

PATTERN USED ....

SUPPLIES NEEDED ....

SKETCH / PHOTO

NOTES

....
....
....
....
....
....
....
....

Sewing Log Book

DETAILS

PROJECT ....

CREATED FOR ....

DATE STARTED .... **DATE COMPLETED** ....

ITEM .... **QTY** ....

PRICE .... **DEPOSIT PAID** .... **BALANCE PAID** ....

PATTERN USED ....

SUPPLIES NEEDED ....

SKETCH / PHOTO

NOTES

....
....
....
....
....
....

Sewing Log Book

DETAILS

PROJECT ....

CREATED FOR ....

DATE STARTED .... **DATE COMPLETED** ....

ITEM .... **QTY** ....

PRICE .... **DEPOSIT PAID** .... **BALANCE PAID** ....

PATTERN USED ....

SUPPLIES NEEDED ....

SKETCH / PHOTO

NOTES

....
....
....
....
....
....
....

Sewing Log Book

DETAILS

PROJECT ....

CREATED FOR ....

DATE STARTED .... DATE COMPLETED ....

ITEM .... QTY ....

PRICE .... DEPOSIT PAID .... BALANCE PAID ....

PATTERN USED ....

SUPPLIES NEEDED ....

SKETCH / PHOTO

NOTES

....
....
....
....
....
....
....
....

Sewing Log Book

DETAILS

PROJECT ....

CREATED FOR ....

DATE STARTED .... **DATE COMPLETED** ....

ITEM .... **QTY** ....

PRICE .... **DEPOSIT PAID** .... **BALANCE PAID** ....

PATTERN USED ....

SUPPLIES NEEDED ....

SKETCH / PHOTO

NOTES

....
....
....
....
....
....
....

Sewing Log Book

DETAILS

PROJECT ....

CREATED FOR ....

DATE STARTED .... DATE COMPLETED ....

ITEM .... QTY ....

PRICE .... DEPOSIT PAID .... BALANCE PAID ....

PATTERN USED ....

SUPPLIES NEEDED ....

SKETCH / PHOTO

NOTES

....
....
....
....
....
....
....
....

Sewing Log Book

DETAILS

PROJECT ....

CREATED FOR ....

DATE STARTED .... DATE COMPLETED ....

ITEM .... QTY ....

PRICE .... DEPOSIT PAID .... BALANCE PAID ....

PATTERN USED ....

SUPPLIES NEEDED ....

SKETCH / PHOTO

NOTES

....
....
....
....
....
....
....

Sewing Log Book

DETAILS

PROJECT ....

CREATED FOR ....

DATE STARTED .... **DATE COMPLETED** ....

ITEM .... **QTY** ....

PRICE .... **DEPOSIT PAID** .... **BALANCE PAID** ....

PATTERN USED ....

SUPPLIES NEEDED ....

SKETCH / PHOTO

NOTES

....
....
....
....
....
....
....

Sewing Log Book

DETAILS

PROJECT ……………………………………………………………………………

CREATED FOR ……………………………………………………………………

DATE STARTED ………………………… DATE COMPLETED ………………………

ITEM ………………………………………………… QTY ………………………

PRICE ………………… DEPOSIT PAID ………………… BALANCE PAID ………………

PATTERN USED ……………………………………………………………………

SUPPLIES NEEDED …………………………………………………………………

SKETCH / PHOTO

NOTES

···
···
···
···
···
···
···

Sewing Log Book

DETAILS

PROJECT ....

CREATED FOR ....

DATE STARTED .... DATE COMPLETED ....

ITEM .... QTY ....

PRICE .... DEPOSIT PAID .... BALANCE PAID ....

PATTERN USED ....

SUPPLIES NEEDED ....

SKETCH / PHOTO

NOTES

....
....
....
....
....
....
....

Sewing Log Book

DETAILS

PROJECT ....

CREATED FOR ....

DATE STARTED .... **DATE COMPLETED** ....

ITEM .... **QTY** ....

PRICE .... **DEPOSIT PAID** .... **BALANCE PAID** ....

PATTERN USED ....

SUPPLIES NEEDED ....

SKETCH / PHOTO

NOTES

....
....
....
....
....
....
....

Sewing Log Book

PROJECT

CREATED FOR

DATE STARTED   DATE COMPLETED

ITEM   QTY

PRICE   DEPOSIT PAID   BALANCE PAID

PATTERN USED

SUPPLIES NEEDED

Sewing Log Book

DETAILS

PROJECT ....

CREATED FOR ....

DATE STARTED .... DATE COMPLETED ....

ITEM .... QTY ....

PRICE .... DEPOSIT PAID .... BALANCE PAID ....

PATTERN USED ....

SUPPLIES NEEDED ....

SKETCH / PHOTO

NOTES

....

....

....

....

....

....

....

Sewing Log Book

DETAILS

PROJECT ....

CREATED FOR ....

DATE STARTED .... DATE COMPLETED ....

ITEM .... QTY ....

PRICE .... DEPOSIT PAID .... BALANCE PAID ....

PATTERN USED ....

SUPPLIES NEEDED ....

SKETCH / PHOTO

NOTES

....
....
....
....
....
....
....

Sewing Log Book

DETAILS

PROJECT ....

CREATED FOR ....

DATE STARTED .... **DATE COMPLETED** ....

ITEM .... **QTY** ....

PRICE .... **DEPOSIT PAID** .... **BALANCE PAID** ....

PATTERN USED ....

SUPPLIES NEEDED ....

SKETCH / PHOTO

NOTES

....
....
....
....
....
....
....

Sewing Log Book

DETAILS

PROJECT ....

CREATED FOR ....

DATE STARTED .... DATE COMPLETED ....

ITEM .... QTY ....

PRICE .... DEPOSIT PAID .... BALANCE PAID ....

PATTERN USED ....

SUPPLIES NEEDED ....

SKETCH / PHOTO

NOTES

....
....
....
....
....
....
....
....

Sewing Log Book

DETAILS

PROJECT ....

CREATED FOR ....

DATE STARTED .... **DATE COMPLETED** ....

ITEM .... **QTY** ....

PRICE .... **DEPOSIT PAID** .... **BALANCE PAID** ....

PATTERN USED ....

SUPPLIES NEEDED ....

SKETCH / PHOTO

NOTES

....
....
....
....
....
....
....

Sewing Log Book

DETAILS

PROJECT ....

CREATED FOR ....

DATE STARTED .... DATE COMPLETED ....

ITEM .... QTY ....

PRICE .... DEPOSIT PAID .... BALANCE PAID ....

PATTERN USED ....

SUPPLIES NEEDED ....

SKETCH / PHOTO

NOTES

....
....
....
....
....
....
....

Sewing Log Book

DETAILS

PROJECT ....

CREATED FOR ....

DATE STARTED .... DATE COMPLETED ....

ITEM .... QTY ....

PRICE .... DEPOSIT PAID .... BALANCE PAID ....

PATTERN USED ....

SUPPLIES NEEDED ....

SKETCH / PHOTO

NOTES

....
....
....
....
....
....
....

Sewing Log Book

DETAILS

PROJECT ....

CREATED FOR ....

DATE STARTED .... DATE COMPLETED ....

ITEM .... QTY ....

PRICE .... DEPOSIT PAID .... BALANCE PAID ....

PATTERN USED ....

SUPPLIES NEEDED ....

SKETCH / PHOTO

NOTES

....
....
....
....
....
....
....

Sewing Log Book

DETAILS

PROJECT ....

CREATED FOR ....

DATE STARTED .... DATE COMPLETED ....

ITEM .... QTY ....

PRICE .... DEPOSIT PAID .... BALANCE PAID ....

PATTERN USED ....

SUPPLIES NEEDED ....

SKETCH / PHOTO

NOTES

....
....
....
....
....
....
....

Sewing Log Book

DETAILS

PROJECT ....

CREATED FOR ....

DATE STARTED .... **DATE COMPLETED** ....

ITEM .... **QTY** ....

PRICE .... **DEPOSIT PAID** .... **BALANCE PAID** ....

PATTERN USED ....

SUPPLIES NEEDED ....

SKETCH / PHOTO

NOTES

....
....
....
....
....
....
....

Sewing Log Book

DETAILS

PROJECT ....

CREATED FOR ....

DATE STARTED .... **DATE COMPLETED** ....

ITEM .... **QTY** ....

PRICE .... **DEPOSIT PAID** .... **BALANCE PAID** ....

PATTERN USED ....

SUPPLIES NEEDED ....

SKETCH / PHOTO

NOTES

....
....
....
....
....
....
....

Sewing Log Book

DETAILS

PROJECT ....

CREATED FOR ....

DATE STARTED .... **DATE COMPLETED** ....

ITEM .... **QTY** ....

PRICE .... **DEPOSIT PAID** .... **BALANCE PAID** ....

PATTERN USED ....

SUPPLIES NEEDED ....

SKETCH / PHOTO

NOTES

....
....
....
....
....
....
....

Sewing Log Book

DETAILS

PROJECT ....

CREATED FOR ....

DATE STARTED .... DATE COMPLETED ....

ITEM .... QTY ....

PRICE .... DEPOSIT PAID .... BALANCE PAID ....

PATTERN USED ....

SUPPLIES NEEDED ....

SKETCH / PHOTO

NOTES

....
....
....
....
....
....
....

Sewing Log Book

DETAILS

PROJECT ....

CREATED FOR ....

DATE STARTED .... DATE COMPLETED ....

ITEM .... QTY ....

PRICE .... DEPOSIT PAID .... BALANCE PAID .....

PATTERN USED ....

SUPPLIES NEEDED ....

SKETCH / PHOTO

NOTES

....
....
....
....
....
....
....

Sewing Log Book

DETAILS

PROJECT ....

CREATED FOR ....

DATE STARTED .... DATE COMPLETED ....

ITEM .... QTY ....

PRICE .... DEPOSIT PAID .... BALANCE PAID ....

PATTERN USED ....

SUPPLIES NEEDED ....

SKETCH / PHOTO

NOTES

....
....
....
....
....
....
....

Sewing Log Book

PROJECT ....

CREATED FOR ....

DATE STARTED .... **DATE COMPLETED** ....

ITEM .... **QTY** ....

PRICE .... **DEPOSIT PAID** .... **BALANCE PAID** ....

PATTERN USED ....

SUPPLIES NEEDED ....

....
....
....
....
....
....
....

Sewing Log Book

DETAILS

PROJECT ....

CREATED FOR ....

DATE STARTED .... **DATE COMPLETED** ....

ITEM .... **QTY** ....

PRICE .... **DEPOSIT PAID** .... **BALANCE PAID** ....

PATTERN USED ....

SUPPLIES NEEDED ....

SKETCH / PHOTO

NOTES

....

....

....

....

....

....

....

Sewing Log Book

DETAILS

PROJECT ....

CREATED FOR ....

DATE STARTED .... DATE COMPLETED ....

ITEM .... QTY ....

PRICE .... DEPOSIT PAID .... BALANCE PAID ....

PATTERN USED ....

SUPPLIES NEEDED ....

SKETCH / PHOTO

NOTES

....
....
....
....
....
....
....

Sewing Log Book

DETAILS

PROJECT ....

CREATED FOR ....

DATE STARTED .... **DATE COMPLETED** ....

ITEM .... **QTY** ....

PRICE .... **DEPOSIT PAID** .... **BALANCE PAID** ....

PATTERN USED ....

SUPPLIES NEEDED ....

SKETCH / PHOTO

NOTES

....
....
....
....
....
....
....

Sewing Log Book

DETAILS

PROJECT ....

CREATED FOR ....

DATE STARTED .... **DATE COMPLETED** ....

ITEM .... **QTY** ....

PRICE .... **DEPOSIT PAID** .... **BALANCE PAID** ....

PATTERN USED ....

SUPPLIES NEEDED ....

SKETCH / PHOTO

NOTES

....
....
....
....
....
....
....
....

Sewing Log Book

DETAILS

PROJECT ....

CREATED FOR ....

DATE STARTED .... DATE COMPLETED ....

ITEM .... QTY ....

PRICE .... DEPOSIT PAID .... BALANCE PAID ....

PATTERN USED ....

SUPPLIES NEEDED ....

SKETCH / PHOTO

NOTES

....
....
....
....
....
....
....

Sewing Log Book

DETAILS

PROJECT ....

CREATED FOR ....

DATE STARTED .... **DATE COMPLETED** ....

ITEM .... **QTY** ....

PRICE .... **DEPOSIT PAID** .... **BALANCE PAID** ....

PATTERN USED ....

SUPPLIES NEEDED ....

SKETCH / PHOTO

NOTES

....
....
....
....
....
....
....
....

Sewing Log Book

DETAILS

PROJECT ....

CREATED FOR ....

DATE STARTED .... **DATE COMPLETED** ....

ITEM .... **QTY** ....

PRICE .... **DEPOSIT PAID** .... **BALANCE PAID** ....

PATTERN USED ....

SUPPLIES NEEDED ....

SKETCH / PHOTO

NOTES

....
....
....
....
....
....
....

Sewing Log Book

DETAILS

PROJECT ....

CREATED FOR ....

DATE STARTED .... **DATE COMPLETED** ....

ITEM .... **QTY** ....

PRICE .... **DEPOSIT PAID** .... **BALANCE PAID** ....

PATTERN USED ....

SUPPLIES NEEDED ....

SKETCH / PHOTO

NOTES

....
....
....
....
....
....
....
....

Sewing Log Book

PROJECT ....

CREATED FOR ....

DATE STARTED .... DATE COMPLETED ....

ITEM .... QTY ....

PRICE .... DEPOSIT PAID .... BALANCE PAID ....

PATTERN USED ....

SUPPLIES NEEDED ....

....

....

....

....

....

....

....

Sewing Log Book

DETAILS

PROJECT ....

CREATED FOR ....

DATE STARTED .... DATE COMPLETED ....

ITEM .... QTY ....

PRICE .... DEPOSIT PAID .... BALANCE PAID ....

PATTERN USED ....

SUPPLIES NEEDED ....

SKETCH / PHOTO

NOTES

....
....
....
....
....
....
....

Sewing Log Book

DETAILS

PROJECT ....

CREATED FOR ....

DATE STARTED .... **DATE COMPLETED** ....

ITEM .... **QTY** ....

PRICE .... **DEPOSIT PAID** .... **BALANCE PAID** ....

PATTERN USED ....

SUPPLIES NEEDED ....

SKETCH / PHOTO

NOTES

....
....
....
....
....
....
....

Sewing Log Book

DETAILS

PROJECT ....

CREATED FOR ....

DATE STARTED .... DATE COMPLETED ....

ITEM .... QTY ....

PRICE .... DEPOSIT PAID .... BALANCE PAID ....

PATTERN USED ....

SUPPLIES NEEDED ....

SKETCH / PHOTO

NOTES

....
....
....
....
....
....
....

Sewing Log Book

PROJECT ....

CREATED FOR ....

DATE STARTED .... **DATE COMPLETED** ....

ITEM .... **QTY** ....

PRICE .... **DEPOSIT PAID** .... **BALANCE PAID** ....

PATTERN USED ....

SUPPLIES NEEDED ....

SKETCH / PHOTO

NOTES

....

....

....

....

....

....

....

Sewing Log Book

DETAILS

PROJECT ....

CREATED FOR ....

DATE STARTED .... **DATE COMPLETED** ....

ITEM .... **QTY** ....

PRICE .... **DEPOSIT PAID** .... **BALANCE PAID** ....

PATTERN USED ....

SUPPLIES NEEDED ....

SKETCH / PHOTO

NOTES

....
....
....
....
....
....
....
....

Sewing Log Book

DETAILS

PROJECT ....

CREATED FOR ....

DATE STARTED .... DATE COMPLETED ....

ITEM .... QTY ....

PRICE .... DEPOSIT PAID .... BALANCE PAID ....

PATTERN USED ....

SUPPLIES NEEDED ....

SKETCH / PHOTO

NOTES

....

....

....

....

....

....

....

Sewing Log Book

DETAILS

PROJECT ……………………………………………………………

CREATED FOR ……………………………………………………

DATE STARTED …………………… **DATE COMPLETED** ……………………

ITEM ……………………………………… **QTY** ……………………

PRICE …………………… **DEPOSIT PAID** …………… **BALANCE PAID** ……………

PATTERN USED …………………………………………………

SUPPLIES NEEDED ………………………………………………

SKETCH / PHOTO

NOTES

………………………………………………………………………
………………………………………………………………………
………………………………………………………………………
………………………………………………………………………
………………………………………………………………………
………………………………………………………………………
………………………………………………………………………

Sewing Log Book

DETAILS

PROJECT ....

CREATED FOR ....

DATE STARTED .... **DATE COMPLETED** ....

ITEM .... **QTY** ....

PRICE .... **DEPOSIT PAID** .... **BALANCE PAID** ....

PATTERN USED ....

SUPPLIES NEEDED ....

SKETCH / PHOTO

NOTES

....
....
....
....
....
....
....

Sewing Log Book

PROJECT ....

CREATED FOR ....

DATE STARTED .... DATE COMPLETED ....

ITEM .... QTY ....

PRICE .... DEPOSIT PAID .... BALANCE PAID ....

PATTERN USED ....

SUPPLIES NEEDED ....

SKETCH / PHOTO

NOTES

....
....
....
....
....
....
....
....

Sewing Log Book

DETAILS

PROJECT ....

CREATED FOR ....

DATE STARTED .... DATE COMPLETED ....

ITEM .... QTY ....

PRICE .... DEPOSIT PAID .... BALANCE PAID ....

PATTERN USED ....

SUPPLIES NEEDED ....

SKETCH / PHOTO

NOTES

....
....
....
....
....
....
....
....

Sewing Log Book

PROJECT ....

CREATED FOR ....

DATE STARTED .... **DATE COMPLETED** ....

ITEM .... **QTY** ....

PRICE .... **DEPOSIT PAID** .... **BALANCE PAID** ....

PATTERN USED ....

SUPPLIES NEEDED ....

....
....
....
....
....
....
....

Sewing Log Book

DETAILS

PROJECT ....

CREATED FOR ....

DATE STARTED .... DATE COMPLETED ....

ITEM .... QTY ....

PRICE .... DEPOSIT PAID .... BALANCE PAID ....

PATTERN USED ....

SUPPLIES NEEDED ....

SKETCH / PHOTO

NOTES

....
....
....
....
....
....
....

Sewing Log Book

DETAILS

PROJECT …………………………………………………………

CREATED FOR …………………………………………………

DATE STARTED …………………… DATE COMPLETED …………………………

ITEM ……………………………………… QTY ……………………

PRICE ………………… DEPOSIT PAID …………… BALANCE PAID ……………

PATTERN USED …………………………………………………

SUPPLIES NEEDED ………………………………………………

SKETCH / PHOTO

NOTES

…………………………………………………………………………
…………………………………………………………………………
…………………………………………………………………………
…………………………………………………………………………
…………………………………………………………………………
…………………………………………………………………………
…………………………………………………………………………

DETAILS

PROJECT ....

CREATED FOR ....

DATE STARTED .... DATE COMPLETED ....

ITEM .... QTY ....

PRICE .... DEPOSIT PAID .... BALANCE PAID ....

PATTERN USED ....

SUPPLIES NEEDED ....

SKETCH / PHOTO

NOTES

....
....
....
....
....
....
....

Sewing Log Book

DETAILS

PROJECT ....

CREATED FOR ....

DATE STARTED .... **DATE COMPLETED** ....

ITEM .... **QTY** ....

PRICE .... **DEPOSIT PAID** .... **BALANCE PAID** ....

PATTERN USED ....

SUPPLIES NEEDED ....

SKETCH / PHOTO

NOTES

....
....
....
....
....
....
....

Sewing Log Book

PROJECT ....

CREATED FOR ....

DATE STARTED .... DATE COMPLETED ....

ITEM .... QTY ....

PRICE .... DEPOSIT PAID .... BALANCE PAID ....

PATTERN USED ....

SUPPLIES NEEDED ....

Sewing Log Book

DETAILS

PROJECT ....

CREATED FOR ....

DATE STARTED .... **DATE COMPLETED** ....

ITEM .... **QTY** ....

PRICE .... **DEPOSIT PAID** .... **BALANCE PAID** ....

PATTERN USED ....

SUPPLIES NEEDED ....

SKETCH / PHOTO

NOTES

....
....
....
....
....
....
....

Sewing Log Book

DETAILS

PROJECT ....

CREATED FOR ....

DATE STARTED .... DATE COMPLETED ....

ITEM .... QTY ....

PRICE .... DEPOSIT PAID .... BALANCE PAID ....

PATTERN USED ....

SUPPLIES NEEDED ....

SKETCH / PHOTO

NOTES

....
....
....
....
....
....
....

DETAILS

PROJECT ....

CREATED FOR ....

DATE STARTED .... **DATE COMPLETED** ....

ITEM .... **QTY** ....

PRICE .... **DEPOSIT PAID** .... **BALANCE PAID** ....

PATTERN USED ....

SUPPLIES NEEDED ....

SKETCH / PHOTO

NOTES

....
....
....
....
....
....
....
....

Sewing Log Book

DETAILS

PROJECT ....

CREATED FOR ....

DATE STARTED .... DATE COMPLETED ....

ITEM .... QTY ....

PRICE .... DEPOSIT PAID .... BALANCE PAID ....

PATTERN USED ....

SUPPLIES NEEDED ....

SKETCH / PHOTO

NOTES

....
....
....
....
....
....
....

Sewing Log Book

DETAILS

PROJECT ....

CREATED FOR ....

DATE STARTED .... DATE COMPLETED ....

ITEM .... QTY ....

PRICE .... DEPOSIT PAID .... BALANCE PAID ....

PATTERN USED ....

SUPPLIES NEEDED ....

SKETCH / PHOTO

NOTES

....
....
....
....
....
....

Sewing Log Book

DETAILS

PROJECT ....

CREATED FOR ....

DATE STARTED .... **DATE COMPLETED** ....

ITEM .... **QTY** ....

PRICE .... **DEPOSIT PAID** .... **BALANCE PAID** ....

PATTERN USED ....

SUPPLIES NEEDED ....

SKETCH / PHOTO

NOTES

....
....
....
....
....
....
....

Sewing Log Book

PROJECT ....

CREATED FOR ....

DATE STARTED .... DATE COMPLETED ....

ITEM .... QTY ....

PRICE .... DEPOSIT PAID .... BALANCE PAID ....

PATTERN USED ....

SUPPLIES NEEDED ....

Sewing Log Book

DETAILS

PROJECT ....

CREATED FOR ....

DATE STARTED .... **DATE COMPLETED** ....

ITEM .... **QTY** ....

PRICE .... **DEPOSIT PAID** .... **BALANCE PAID** ....

PATTERN USED ....

SUPPLIES NEEDED ....

SKETCH / PHOTO

NOTES

....
....
....
....
....
....
....

Sewing Log Book

DETAILS

PROJECT ....

CREATED FOR ....

DATE STARTED .... DATE COMPLETED ....

ITEM .... QTY ....

PRICE .... DEPOSIT PAID .... BALANCE PAID ....

PATTERN USED ....

SUPPLIES NEEDED ....

SKETCH / PHOTO

NOTES

....
....
....
....
....
....
....

Sewing Log Book

DETAILS

PROJECT ....

CREATED FOR ....

DATE STARTED .... DATE COMPLETED ....

ITEM .... QTY ....

PRICE .... DEPOSIT PAID .... BALANCE PAID ....

PATTERN USED ....

SUPPLIES NEEDED ....

SKETCH / PHOTO

NOTES

....
....
....
....
....
....
....

Sewing Log Book

DETAILS

PROJECT ....

CREATED FOR ....

DATE STARTED .... DATE COMPLETED ....

ITEM .... QTY ....

PRICE .... DEPOSIT PAID .... BALANCE PAID ....

PATTERN USED ....

SUPPLIES NEEDED ....

SKETCH / PHOTO

NOTES

....
....
....
....
....
....
....

Sewing Log Book

PROJECT ....

CREATED FOR ....

DATE STARTED .... DATE COMPLETED ....

ITEM .... QTY ....

PRICE .... DEPOSIT PAID .... BALANCE PAID ....

PATTERN USED ....

SUPPLIES NEEDED ....

Sewing Log Book

DETAILS

PROJECT ....

CREATED FOR ....

DATE STARTED .... DATE COMPLETED ....

ITEM .... QTY ....

PRICE .... DEPOSIT PAID .... BALANCE PAID ....

PATTERN USED ....

SUPPLIES NEEDED ....

SKETCH / PHOTO

NOTES

....

....

....

....

....

....

....

....

Sewing Log Book

PROJECT ....

CREATED FOR ....

DATE STARTED .... DATE COMPLETED ....

ITEM .... QTY ....

PRICE .... DEPOSIT PAID .... BALANCE PAID ....

PATTERN USED ....

SUPPLIES NEEDED ....

....
....
....
....
....
....
....
....

Sewing Log Book

DETAILS

PROJECT ....

CREATED FOR ....

DATE STARTED .... **DATE COMPLETED** ....

ITEM .... **QTY** ....

PRICE .... **DEPOSIT PAID** .... **BALANCE PAID** ....

PATTERN USED ....

SUPPLIES NEEDED ....

SKETCH / PHOTO

NOTES

....

....

....

....

....

....

....

Sewing Log Book

DETAILS

PROJECT ....

CREATED FOR ....

DATE STARTED .... DATE COMPLETED ....

ITEM .... QTY ....

PRICE .... DEPOSIT PAID .... BALANCE PAID ....

PATTERN USED ....

SUPPLIES NEEDED ....

SKETCH / PHOTO

NOTES

....
....
....
....
....
....
....

Sewing Log Book

DETAILS

PROJECT ....

CREATED FOR ....

DATE STARTED .... DATE COMPLETED ....

ITEM .... QTY ....

PRICE .... DEPOSIT PAID .... BALANCE PAID ....

PATTERN USED ....

SUPPLIES NEEDED ....

SKETCH / PHOTO

NOTES

....
....
....
....
....
....

Sewing Log Book

DETAILS

PROJECT ....

CREATED FOR ....

DATE STARTED .... DATE COMPLETED ....

ITEM .... QTY ....

PRICE .... DEPOSIT PAID .... BALANCE PAID ....

PATTERN USED ....

SUPPLIES NEEDED ....

SKETCH / PHOTO

NOTES

....
....
....
....
....
....
....

Sewing Log Book

DETAILS

PROJECT ....

CREATED FOR ....

DATE STARTED .... DATE COMPLETED ....

ITEM .... QTY ....

PRICE .... DEPOSIT PAID .... BALANCE PAID ....

PATTERN USED ....

SUPPLIES NEEDED ....

SKETCH / PHOTO

NOTES

....
....
....
....
....
....
....

Sewing Log Book

DETAILS

PROJECT ....

CREATED FOR ....

DATE STARTED .... DATE COMPLETED ....

ITEM .... QTY ....

PRICE .... DEPOSIT PAID .... BALANCE PAID ....

PATTERN USED ....

SUPPLIES NEEDED ....

SKETCH / PHOTO

NOTES

....
....
....
....
....
....
....

Sewing Log Book

PROJECT ....

CREATED FOR ....

DATE STARTED .... **DATE COMPLETED** ....

ITEM .... **QTY** ....

PRICE .... **DEPOSIT PAID** .... **BALANCE PAID** ....

PATTERN USED ....

SUPPLIES NEEDED ....

....
....
....
....
....
....
....

Sewing Log Book

DETAILS

PROJECT ....

CREATED FOR ....

DATE STARTED .... DATE COMPLETED ....

ITEM .... QTY ....

PRICE .... DEPOSIT PAID .... BALANCE PAID ....

PATTERN USED ....

SUPPLIES NEEDED ....

SKETCH / PHOTO

NOTES

....

....

....

....

....

....

....

Sewing Log Book

DETAILS

PROJECT ....

CREATED FOR ....

DATE STARTED .... DATE COMPLETED ....

ITEM .... QTY ....

PRICE .... DEPOSIT PAID .... BALANCE PAID ....

PATTERN USED ....

SUPPLIES NEEDED ....

SKETCH / PHOTO

NOTES

....
....
....
....
....
....
....

Sewing Log Book

PROJECT ....

CREATED FOR ....

DATE STARTED .... DATE COMPLETED ....

ITEM .... QTY ....

PRICE .... DEPOSIT PAID .... BALANCE PAID ....

PATTERN USED ....

SUPPLIES NEEDED ....

....
....
....
....
....
....
....

Sewing Log Book

DETAILS

PROJECT ....

CREATED FOR ....

DATE STARTED .... DATE COMPLETED ....

ITEM .... QTY ....

PRICE .... DEPOSIT PAID .... BALANCE PAID ....

PATTERN USED ....

SUPPLIES NEEDED ....

SKETCH / PHOTO

NOTES

....
....
....
....
....
....
....

Sewing Log Book

DETAILS

PROJECT ....

CREATED FOR ....

DATE STARTED .... DATE COMPLETED ....

ITEM .... QTY ....

PRICE .... DEPOSIT PAID .... BALANCE PAID ....

PATTERN USED ....

SUPPLIES NEEDED ....

SKETCH / PHOTO

NOTES

....

....

....

....

....

....

....

Sewing Log Book

PROJECT ....

CREATED FOR ....

DATE STARTED .... **DATE COMPLETED** ....

ITEM .... **QTY** ....

PRICE .... **DEPOSIT PAID** .... **BALANCE PAID** ....

PATTERN USED ....

SUPPLIES NEEDED ....

....
....
....
....
....
....
....

DETAILS

PROJECT ....

CREATED FOR ....

DATE STARTED .... DATE COMPLETED ....

ITEM .... QTY ....

PRICE .... DEPOSIT PAID .... BALANCE PAID ....

PATTERN USED ....

SUPPLIES NEEDED ....

SKETCH / PHOTO

NOTES

....

....

....

....

....

....

....

Sewing Log Book

DETAILS

PROJECT ....

CREATED FOR ....

DATE STARTED .... DATE COMPLETED ....

ITEM .... QTY ....

PRICE .... DEPOSIT PAID .... BALANCE PAID ....

PATTERN USED ....

SUPPLIES NEEDED ....

SKETCH / PHOTO

NOTES

....
....
....
....
....
....
....

Sewing Log Book

DETAILS

PROJECT ....

CREATED FOR ....

DATE STARTED .... DATE COMPLETED ....

ITEM .... QTY ....

PRICE .... DEPOSIT PAID .... BALANCE PAID ....

PATTERN USED ....

SUPPLIES NEEDED ....

SKETCH / PHOTO

NOTES

....
....
....
....
....
....
....

Sewing Log Book

DETAILS

PROJECT ....

CREATED FOR ....

DATE STARTED .... DATE COMPLETED ....

ITEM .... QTY ....

PRICE .... DEPOSIT PAID .... BALANCE PAID ....

PATTERN USED ....

SUPPLIES NEEDED ....

SKETCH / PHOTO

NOTES

....
....
....
....
....
....
....